C000150540

i puffin
love you

HarperCollins*Publishers*
1 London Bridge Street
London SE1 9GF

www.harpercollins.co.uk

First published by HarperCollins*Publishers* 2021

1 3 5 7 9 10 8 6 4 2

Text © HarperCollins*Publishers* 2021
Illustrations © Lydia Kairl

HarperCollins*Publishers* asserts the moral right to be
identified as the author of this work

A catalogue record of this book is
available from the British Library

ISBN 978-0-00-845554-5

Printed and bound in Latvia

MIX
Paper from
responsible sources
FSC™ C007454

This book is produced from independently certified FSC™ paper to
ensure responsible forest management.

For more information visit: www.harpercollins.co.uk/green

i puffin love you

hilarious animal puns
to help you share the love

HarperCollins*Publishers*

Hey, corgeous!

Some-bunny
really loves
you

You're my most
significant otter

A toucan of my affection

I chews you

You are
dino-mite

I wallaby by
your side

You're the
bear-y
best

I'm nuts
about you

You're
udder-ly
perfect

You always
octo-py
my thoughts

Life without you
would be ruff

You're the swan
for me

I love spending
koala-ty time
together

Thank you for
owl-ways
being there for me

You are absolutely
dove-ly

I am very
fawn-ed of you,
my deer

We bee-long
together

Everything else is
irr-elephant when
I'm with you

I love you
and rhino you
love me too

You're shrimp-ly
the best

You are toad-ally amazing

I love hanging
out with you

Ewe complete me

You give my life
porpoise

You never bug me

I hippopota-miss
you when you're
away

I'd be lion if I said
I didn't love you

You're my
sole-mate

I love our
hedge-hugs

We just clicked

I want to panda to
your every need

You hold the kiwi
to my heart

I love you an
axo-lot-l

When we first met,
I gnu you were the
one for me

You're always so
emu-sing

Life's snow fun
without you

You are turtle-y
adorable

You croc my world

I love you pig
time

You turn my
heart to jelly

Are you a beaver?
Because dam!

I'm so glad
I've goat you

You really are my
prime mate

We go so whale together

You give me
goosebumps

I porcu-pine for you when I'm not with you

That's a whole
lobster love

I'm head over
eels for you

We're tweet-hearts

You're so foxy

Kiss me quack

I moose you when
we're apart

You are one in
a chameleon

Waddle I do without you?

I labr-adore
you

I will always
kanga-root
for you

May our love never
tapir off

Llama love you
forever

You're
roar-some

You've got my
seal of approval

Always yours,
meow and forever